The Lost Girls:

a poetry collection on girlhood, grief and growing up

The Lost Girls:
a poetry collection on girlhood, grief and growing up

LYRA WREN

THE OUTSIDER **POET PRESS**

Baltimore, Maryland

The Outsider Poet Press
@outsiderpoetpress
outsiderpoetpress.com

ISBN: 978-1-959373-11-7

Cover and Book Design by Keller Makemson
@kmakemson.design
kmakemson.com

To the lost ones trying to find their way

*And to my family who gifted me
my love for the stars.
I would not be who I am if not for you
and for that, thank you.*

She was a soft-hearted thing
born to a cruel world which
sought to harden her. And yet,
she loved so deeply that when
they begged her to temper the sun,
she'd do it with teeth bared
against the burn and insist
that it warmed her.

Contents

Trigger Warning

This book contains topics related to:

- ✦ mental health issues
- ✦ eating disorders
- ✦ self harm
- ✦ homophobia

The Beginning

LYRA WREN

The child began as a flame igniting
in her mother's womb. A young girl
fighting her way into a world that
assumed it could snuff her out as she grew.
Her unruliness was rejected
and she was deemed to be too much.
Still, she wore rebellion on her chest.
One look into her eyes and you knew
she'd burn this world to the ground.

THE LOST GIRLS

She'd been a little wild child
who didn't think much about her looks.
Too busy soaking up sunshine
to worry about the knots in her hair.
Knees always bruised and clothes wrinkled
from running around. She was ravenous
for things that every girl starves for:
independence, adventure and mischief.
Unkempt and unattainable while girlhood
demanded she satisfy her hunger
for identity in a world constantly trying
to tell her who she is supposed to be.

LYRA WREN

I am nostalgic for childhood.
For the late evenings spent
capturing fireflies in our cupped palms
when we pressed them to our cheeks
to whisper our wishes.
The sound of cicadas buzzing was the
soundtrack to summers left long behind.
Days were spent ankle-deep in the creek
on the green belt, chasing after crawdads.
Sleepovers with siblings where we giggled
in the dark, unaware of the years
leaking away between our fingers.

THE LOST GIRLS

When I was a baby I had a stuffed piglet
twice the size of me and as I grew bigger
he grew smaller because of how hard
I would squeeze. He held me close
each night at bed and wiped my tears
when I felt sad. He listened to my stories
and dreams of who I wanted to be.
He was the perfect companion to me.
To be loved is to be changed and years later,
neither of us are the same.
The stuffing in his body has flattened
and he is now dirty and worn down
but I loved him then and I love him now.

LYRA WREN

Being sisters means you'll peel
the rinds of your oranges
and while the smell of citrus
saturates the air,
you'll find yourself handing
over half for an equal share.
Because being siblings means
willingly going half hungry
to share in life's sweetness.

THE LOST GIRLS

My favorite summer mornings were spent
with the curtains fluttering around the frame
of my bedroom window.
Just cracked open to hear the coo
of the mourning dove.
Our grandmother's woven baskets
hung from our hands,
a call to compete for who could
collect the most blackberries from the garden.
The berries burst sourly beneath my tongue
a contrast to sweet childhood summers.

I have fond memories of vacations
with my family. Sitting in a cramped car
for hours while my siblings and I
begged for the gas station's $1 slurpees.
The destinations were always fun,
don't get me wrong, but the in-betweens
were my favorite part. The games we'd play
on the way and the inside jokes we'd make.
Sharing beds with sisters and staying awake
for far too late. Things were easier then,
back when I was carefree, but for the rest of my life
nostalgia will taste like cherry and petroleum to me.

THE LOST GIRLS

There is something peaceful
about the car ride home after a trip.
Laying drowsily in my car seat
while my fingers traced the rain
racing down the windowpane.
Eventually I'd surrender myself to sleep
because even with my eyes closed
I was confident in where I was going.
I knew I'd be home soon.

LYRA WREN

To my childhood best friend,

I miss being gremlin girls
always hiding in the woods.
Climbing trees and scratching up
our knees, wearing our bruises
with pride and wide grins.
We linked our pinkies and swore
that we would be friends forever.
It's the only promise I've ever broken.
Nothing happened. We didn't fight.
We just grew up and grew apart.
Even so, you made a mark in my life
and you will always matter to me.

THE LOST GIRLS

As a child, there was magic
in the mundane.
I miss seeing mermaids
among the koi in the pond,
their glittering scales reminiscent
of a childhood fairytale.
Summer mornings I'd make bouquets
out of the same flowers
adults would mow away while
wrinkling their noses at the weeds.
And I wonder when the awe
of the day to day faded away
and when we stopped believing
in our own ability to see mermaids
in the monotonous world around us.

LYRA WREN

To my mom,

When the teacher asked me
what I wanted to be someday
I could never choose.
Did I want to be an artist? A writer?
An actress? Or even a singer? But with certainty,
my answer was always you.
I wanted to love just as gently
and make people warm with my smile.
I wanted to be there for others
and go the extra mile.
In my mind, my mom is the prettiest,
the wisest and the kindest person.
She is all of these things
and all I ever wanted
was to be that too.

THE LOST GIRLS

The first time a woman smiled at me
and butterflies rose in my stomach,
I felt like sin personified. My lips
pressed together and I tried to swallow
the feeling down, knowing that if
I spoke it out loud, I couldn't take it back.
Damn this society for turning the elation
of a girl's first crush into quiet shame.

LYRA WREN

The best thing my father gifted me
was my love for the stars.
Each meteor shower, he would
pull my family out to the lawn and
we'd spread the blankets across
the grass and lie there in awe.
He'd point out the planets and
teach me new facts, all of which
left me wide-eyed and feeling small.
There was no red, hot rage or fear
nor eyes glassy with tears. There was
only a fondness for family and soft
quiet contemplation. I just wish these
nights could have lasted forever.

THE LOST GIRLS

Sisters carry a sense of solidarity.
I know that they will be by my side
no matter how hard life may be.
They will help me build bridges,
but if the wood begins to rot,
threatening to collapse beneath my feet
then they will be there with the matches.
And if those bridges should burn,
they will be there to help me rebuild.

LYRA WREN

When she was a little girl
she captured fireflies
in an old glass jar
and swore she held
the stars in her hands.
And what a lovely thing it was
to grasp the cosmos
here on earth and believe
the stars knew your secrets.

THE LOST GIRLS

Universes have been made
from the stardust in my veins.
I taste the metal on my tongue
while the iron in my blood sings,
you are a love child of the cosmos:
never assume you are anything less.

LYRA WREN

The little wild girl lived
in her grandmother's garden.
Always listening to the hum
of the bees while barefoot
in a sea of petals.
Sweat glinted on her brow and
her clothes were muddied but
she was at home in her chaotic kingdom.
She was a girl with sunflowers for eyes.
Hardy and headstrong. Remaining optimistic
even in the toughest of times.
I only wish I could have prevented
that light from leaving her gaze.

THE LOST GIRLS

I learned early that
anger was protection.
A shield built of barbed tongues
and salt-covered wounds.
I am the eldest daughter
who inherited anger issues
from her father and anger
was our love language.
Every tear-stained cheek
and wobbly mouth a sign of affection
that I accepted with an unrelenting thirst.
I craved his approval so much
that I lapped up the violence
and made it an act of love.

Are you ever afraid of living
in your little world alone?
The stars ask of the girl sitting
in her windowsill. She watches them
twinkle in quiet contemplation.

"No," she admits with a soft smile.
"Being awake is far lonelier."

THE LOST GIRLS

The dove's wings were clipped
and she was released to earth
where she could live a mortal life.
Though she was grounded by gravity,
each night she gazed at the stars,
eyes wide with wonder, and she flew.

LYRA WREN

Peter pan led the lost boys but what
of the lost girls? The ones forced to
grow up too quick. Even Wendy Darling
with all her wit was only a girl when she fled
to Neverland, straight into the confinement
of motherhood. Punished because she yearned
for childhood again. She must have forgotten
that young girls are spoon-fed responsibility.
Made to swallow their righteous rage because
boys simply do not know better. Girls hunger to be
heard and understood. They sharpen their tongues
only to bite their words down because it is unseemly
for them to lie bleeding. No one speaks of the lost girls,
but what becomes of them when they have no leader?

THE LOST GIRLS

When I was young, society decided to settle
a blanket of mediocrity around my shoulders.
And what a weight it was, believing myself to be
an agent of averageness at the tender age of twelve.
What fear I felt when I became convinced that
my longing for a world beyond daily life
was already unattainable.

LYRA WREN

A girl on the school bus sits
with her bag and faded barbie
lunchbox lovingly packed.
She is perched on the cusp of
adolescence but her girlhood
hangs on. She rubs her thumb
on the peeling logo while she remembers
scabbed knees and calloused hands.
Preferring pink and purple and wishing
she could splash the colors on the
walls of her room. She's traded Coca Cola
flavored lip smackers for her favorite
cherry lip gloss and a sense of sadness
and nostalgia washes over her. For what
is girlhood but grief and glory.

THE LOST GIRLS

They will tell lost girls to find their own way,
placing an atlas in the palm of their hand.
But they still insist that there's a correct path to take
– that if you make one mistake, you'll be ruined for life.
After awhile, your fire and hunger for independence
are overtaken by insecurities and it becomes easier
to listen to those who criticize your dreams.
You begin to think that following the directions
of others is safer and you begin to forget that
you ever had your own taste for adventure.

LYRA WREN

Girlhood is bubblegum pink and skinned knees
the color of the Pepto Bismol we take for each
anxiety induced stomachache. It is being told
that silence is kindness and good girls are polite to
the boys who harass them on the playground
because in truth, it's just proof that "they like you."
It's sharpie flowers drawn on the inside of your arm
and applying glitter to your cheeks but calling it stars.
It's mascara-rimmed eyes from the lonely, late nights
where all you can do is lie there and cry. It's female rage
willfully dampened by softness and sadness because
girls will always grow into weary women.

The Becoming

LYRA WREN

A girl wrapped thorns
around her fingertips
hoping to grow roses
for the people around her.
When the petals blended
with her blood they made
for the loveliest red but
when the time came that
she reached for another's hand
she was readily rejected
and still, she bled.

THE LOST GIRLS

The first man in my life
taught me to be terrified
of others like him.
Whenever I wept he told me
not to cry or he'd give me
something to cry about.
And so I learned to swallow
the sadness and turned it to
anger instead. They did always say
I was just like my dad.

Dear girl with the 'cat scratches,'

I think about you all the time.
About how lonely you must be.
Crying into your pillow each night,
always alone because nobody else
is there to dry them for you. But at 3 a.m
when your hollow gaze is locked to your ceiling,
remember the others who look upward
wishing they could be somewhere else.
Someone else. And know you're not alone.

THE LOST GIRLS

They beg you to light up the room
with your smile
and you've always been a people pleaser
so you shine and shine
and shine
until all you have left to hold
is an empty matchbox.

LYRA WREN

To my ex best friend,

Today someone asked me if I knew you
and my chest hurt knowing I used to.
We were once a perfect duo,
swearing we were soulmates
— even siblings in another life.
And it could have been fate
or maybe we just drifted apart,
an inexplicable emptiness
seating itself between our souls,
and the worst part of all
is you're the first one I want to text
when the pain of missing you
aches like an open wound.
You will always know me
but you are just a stranger now.

THE LOST GIRLS

Sometimes I like to play pretend.
I'll dress up as a happy girl and
wear a wide grin while I try to
ease perfection over the crevices
of my constantly cracking foundation.
I begin to think that maybe if I wear
enough lip gloss and grit, I'll shift
into someone a little more lovable.
But it's like I'm always waiting for the
other shoe to drop. As if it's inevitable
that I'll sink back into my empty shell.
My happiness is not part of some fallacy
and yet some days I'm fully convinced
that all I am is my sadness.

LYRA WREN

They say failure helps you grow
but they must not know about the
promises of disappointment
waiting for you back home.
Failure has always sat like lead
in my stomach, poisoning me
with broken pieces of pride.
My fear of imperfection is in
the shape of my father when
he coldly tells me to try harder
but what do you do when your best
just isn't good enough?

THE LOST GIRLS

They call you a daydreamer.
A forager of thoughts.
Too mysterious to exist
in just one universe.
But I've never seen mystery
look so sad before and I wonder
if maybe you dream of other worlds
to escape this one.

LYRA WREN

She asks me why I spend my days
in bed but how do I tell the woman
who gave birth to me that it's because
I only smile in my sleep.

THE LOST GIRLS

Society is a siren luring us in with
unkept promises and false ideals.
Glossy magazine covers endorsed
by models who have been photoshopped
and *fixed* will claim that the newest fad diet
will get you the body of your dreams.
There are children who step on the scale
and weep while their parents wonder why
they said they weren't hungry tonight.
Starvation has been glorified and in some cases
encouraged but there is nothing beautiful in
trying to find fulfillment in an empty stomach.

LYRA WREN

In my dreams a younger version of me
sits in the passenger seat of my beat-up Honda.
The traffic lights shine green at the intersection
ahead of me but without much thinking I slam
on my brakes. Though her body jerks forward
and though it must hurt when the seat belt bruises
her skin, she turns to me with placid eyes.
her tiny hand pats my knee and she smiles.

"Are you afraid?" She asks.

"I-I don't know."

"Do you stop at every green light you see?"

I don't answer but somehow she knows.
(She always knows)

"Let's keep going." She says it like a promise.

So we drive.

THE LOST GIRLS

There is an enemy inside my head.
She cradles me closely whispering
false promises of protection.
Do not move. Do not breathe.
Do not embarrass yourself.
She drowns me beneath the echo
of insecurity and I try to escape inside
the safety of the bathroom.
Under the flicker of the fluorescent lights,
I stare into the mirror,
and glare at her sallow face.
Stop it. Please just stop it.
And anxiety will swear,
I am only trying to protect you.
And anxiety will whisper,
you are your own worst enemy.

LYRA WREN

One night you sat on your windowsill
and made confessions to the cosmos.
"I've been cursed with a bleeding heart."

Is that truly a curse? The moon asked.
Its light caressed your cheeks, making
your tears glint like stars.

"I am tired of being wounded," you wept.

The moon considered this then whispered,
some go through life with hardened hearts
but don't you think that's rather lonely?
Be proud when they make you bleed because
to feel. To trust. To love. That is to be human.

THE LOST GIRLS

When you choose to love someone
you make a vow with the universe,
an unspoken promise that one day
this love is going to cause you pain.
Because to know love is to know grief.
To say hello, you will one day have to
say goodbye. When it hurts love feels
like a curse and I wonder why I would
subject myself to this misery but by God,
if it isn't worth it every time.

LYRA WREN

Children grow up trapped within
the confines of a glass house whose
walls tremble with their parents' rage.
At an early age, they learn to swallow
the lump that sits at the back of their throat,
fearful that if they make a sound the very
foundation will crack beneath their feet
and it will be all of their fault.

THE LOST GIRLS

I never knew what it meant
to be soft. Not when anger
burned itself into my DNA.
Not when I grew up in a world
engulfed by flames where all
I could do was choke on the ashes
of what humanity could have been.

One night my dad and I sat
side by side, staring up at the stars.
And without hesitation, I whispered,
"I don't think you're a good person."

"And you are?" He asked quietly.

"No. I'm too much like you for that."

THE LOST GIRLS

It would have been a kinder fate
if you had stolen my words,
but you did not stop there
– you brutalized them.
Making sure that even
when I got them back
they would never forget
the torture of being vulnerable
with someone.

LYRA WREN

She'd made herself untouchable
but deep down she longed to feel
someone else's arms wrapped around her.
Sometimes at night she closed her eyes
and clasped her hands tightly
on either shoulder, trying to imagine
if this is what it would *feel like*
to have a person to hold her.
She hoped it was warmer than this.

THE LOST GIRLS

I've always been a hopeless romantic
and yet, when someone looks at me with
intention heavy in their eyes, I freeze.
My heart flutters in my chest and I pull back.
I think it's because in stories I know there is
a happy ending. I know that the characters
will just click in some inexplicable way.
That somehow they will just get each other
in a manner that no one else can. But this isn't
a story. It's real. And I just can't imagine
a world in which I'm anyone's number one.

LYRA WREN

Everytime a boy caresses my cheek
and insists that I am not like other girls
I flinch at the implication that my form
of femininity was made for his amusement.
I do not spend my days molding myself
to meet his standards and my interests
were not fabricated so he could be my prize.
Don't you dare put me on a pedestal while
damning my gender. I am *just* like other girls
so cast me with the wretched creatures
you call woman.

THE LOST GIRLS

People always wonder why
I cry on each birthday.
Why I don a black dress to
celebrate another year gone by.
But it always made sense to me
because goodbyes are hard and so
I'll blow out the candles and bury her.

My first kiss was with a girl
at a sleepover. We reassured
each other in hushed whispers
that this was only a 'practice kiss.'
Her cherry kisses made my stomach
flutter but fear imprinted illusions
of sin in the back of my mind and
I think we both were afraid to admit
what it would mean if it was real.

THE LOST GIRLS

Tomorrow is my high school graduation.
I will walk across a stage and away
from the people I've always known.
But tonight, my friends and I sit
on the edge of a dock, watching
the ever-present moonlight
ripple across the water.
Despite whispered promises of forever
part of me knows that within a day,
something will change.
Tomorrow I will graduate.
In two months I leave for a university
that none of my friends will be attending.
But tonight, I'll sear the sound
of their laughter into my mind
and hold onto them a little longer.

LYRA WREN

I have many happy memories but
some of my favorite nights were laughing
with my high school friends until my ribs hurt
and tears spilled from my eyes. I cried just as hard
the day we went our separate ways,
wishing we could go back to being teenagers
when we could see each other every day.
But you're my best friends and no matter
how far the distance between us may be
you'll always hold a piece of home for me.

THE LOST GIRLS

I think part of me will always
be stuck at eighteen.
Dreaming of adulthood
through a rose-colored screen.
I thought maybe I'd find
where I was meant to be.
But mostly, I just feel lost
and homesick for a home
I'm not sure I'll ever see.

LYRA WREN

I wish I could talk to my younger self.
I'd gaze at her naive smile and starlit eyes,
bitterness welling in my chest when I think
of the pain she will go through.
How her eyes will grow dull.
My hands look too small to carry
that weight and yet they do.
But still, I'd kneel before her
and with tears in my eyes,
I'd hold her close to my chest
and I would whisper, "I'm sorry."

THE LOST GIRLS

In my memories a younger version of me
sits on a merry-go-round. She's chosen the
white horse with the chipped paint and faded colors
but it gleams brightly beneath the flashing lights
(it almost looks like stars)
and maybe that's why she loved it so much.

But she goes around again. And again. And again.
And I begin to feel sick.

"Why don't we get off the carousel?" I suggest.
I know it will not change anything.

"Why would I?" She asks.
"It's taking me where I need to go."

"It's going nowhere." I whisper. It's going nowhere good.

"We're going somewhere." She says pointedly.

We're not, I thought desperately with tears in my eyes.
We're not but still we continued.

LYRA WREN

People mock my generation: gen z,
The ones who cry far too easily.
Sensitive kids who can't take a joke.
Too young. Too dumb. Too misguided.
We were born beneath no grandeur illusions,
rebellion as our daily bread and butter.
We find no comfort in the status quo so
we dare to ask, how can we do better?
Let them demean us. Let them call us soft.
Because yes, we may weep and feel freely
but when we hurt, we hurt together.
We practice empathy as we hold each other high.
I love the way we live. I love the way we love.

THE LOST GIRLS

I cannot bring myself to confess
that I am lonely because if I say it
out loud, any attention after echoes
of false pity. Instead I cower in the quiet
of my room and let the unbearable feeling
knock the breath from my lungs. I gasp
for something that is just out of reach.
I'm sick and tired of writing about loneliness
but rarely do I identify with anything else.

LYRA WREN

The north star has led humanity
for centuries, but never me.
Everytime I look into the sky
hoping for some sort of sign,
I'm left with a clouded mind
and thoughts tinged with anxiety.
I just want somebody to guide me
out of this lost and lonely feeling.

The Breaking

LYRA WREN

The girl was soft-hearted and smooth as sea glass.
Her surface still, like a crystal clear pool.
They didn't know about the years she spent
tumbling beneath turbulent waves until
sand scraped her soul and salt water
stung her eyes. They didn't know how much
violence she endured to become this gentle.

THE LOST GIRLS

My parents were high school sweethearts
and to me, they always represented
the perfect love story. Maybe I was naive
in thinking we were a happy family.
That I would never be a child of divorce.
But it wasn't meant to be.
50% of children will witness the end
of their parent's marriage. But not me. Never me.
That's what I wanted to think but
this fairytale fantasy I had of them in my mind
crumbled right before my eyes and I couldn't
deny it then. No matter how hard I tried.

LYRA WREN

As a child I was loud, proud
and unapologetic about my opinions.
Extroverted and unafraid and yet
somewhere along the way
the words became caught in my throat.
I think too much before I speak
and then say nothing at all.
I cocoon myself beneath my blankets
creating a wall between me and outside eyes.
I've become a secondary character
in my own story and I don't know how
to pick up the pen again.

THE LOST GIRLS

Tears didn't drip down
her cheeks like diamonds.
And nobody was there to lovingly
brush the wetness from her face.
She often cried in the dark, alone
accompanied only by the sobs
hitching in her chest.
Sometimes she'd stare at the
sorry sight in the mirror.
And if she looked long enough,
she could pretend she was
someone else entirely.

LYRA WREN

I don't know who I am
when I am not sad.
Depression has damned me
for so long that happiness
makes me feel like a
foreigner in my own body.

THE LOST GIRLS

Depression is not a gaping wound
but an emptiness that sits heavy
in your chest. It is a parasite leeching
the optimism from your blood until
it feels as if it was never there at all.
Until it feels as if it will never be there again.
The devastation of your own mind
becoming your enemy is heartbreaking.
It is *heartbreaking* to believe that nobody
in this world loves you when the opposite
is true. It is a tragedy when you cannot find
love for yourself because a disease has
made it an impossibility. Depression is not
a gaping wound. It is a paradox. It is the
heaviest emptiness in this universe.

LYRA WREN

I'm not a little girl anymore
but I still chase dreams of
the father I could have had.
Childhood memories are tainted
by my tears and his rage and
all these years later, he has yet
to change. As I age, I've accepted
that he is the dad I was meant to have
but younger me will always flinch away
so how can I forgive him?

THE LOST GIRLS

Nothing in the fridge
could fill the void
that has settled in the
pit of my stomach
But it does not stop me
from cramming food
down my throat hoping
to find fulfillment.

LYRA WREN

What do I write about when my feelings
are too big for the confinement of words.
When I know that no pretty metaphors
will make my pain more palatable.
Maybe I'll mention that some days I am
a stranger in my own skin or maybe
talk about how I feel like an imitation
of what a human being is supposed to be.
I could keep it soft and admit that pink
is my favorite color because sadness
can't seem to touch it or I could confess
that I always play music because silence
is the most deafening noise but no matter
how many platitudes I use to decorate
this emptiness, the reality remains that
depression just really f*cking sucks.

THE LOST GIRLS

Do not romanticize
the bruises beneath my eyes.
Do not compare them
to fields of lilacs
ready to be plucked.
I'm just tired.
I'm just so goddamn tired.
And there's nothing beautiful
about that.

The ground is reassuringly solid.
When I am overthinking and
the thoughts circle through the
labyrinth inside of my head,
I sink down to my bedroom carpet
and sigh with relief as my back
hits the floor. Because instead
of falling lower (as I could go no further)
The thread of hope inside my chest
can only tread up from here.
What goes down must come up but
I think I'll lie here a little longer.

THE LOST GIRLS

The therapist's office was small.
It didn't seem large enough to house
the weight of a person's woes.
But here I sat, with anger bubbling
beneath my skin and the room
was still standing, unscathed.

"So, why are you here?" They always ask that.

"I feel like I'm poisoning the people I love."
I'm full of restless rage and regret.

"Anger is only a demand to be heard."
She smiles and I flinch in the face of her empathy.

"It is neither good nor bad but when you're
silent and bleeding, anger is a call for healing."

The room was bleak. The therapist, unassuming.
But somehow, I left feeling a little bit lighter.

LYRA WREN

Blood is thicker than water.
Her father's anger runs through
her veins. Her mother's misery
mars her face. When they hurt her
they think she will stay but
does it matter if blood is thicker
than water when she lies bleeding
from the wounds they gave.

THE LOST GIRLS

There are echoes of you in every
man I see and I think that's why
I find them so untrustworthy.
You made me a touch-starved tragedy
and it's because of you that I'm still
learning how to hold hands instead
of clenching my fists in anger.

The moon's beauty cannot be captured
in its entirety through the lens of a camera.
So whenever I see you stare at your picture
and wrinkle your nose in disgust,
I pity the camera for never seeing you
through my eyes because each snapshot
of you is truly a masterpiece.

THE LOST GIRLS

Darling close your eyes
and kiss me because you taste
like the salvation I've been seeking.
You didn't rescue me and act
as my knight in shining armor
but each time your hand is in mine
I am a little less lonely
and that matters most of all.

LYRA WREN

Honeyed lies of love dripped from your tongue,
curdling sourly in the pit of my stomach.
But I swallowed down the acidity,
craving your deceptions because it meant
you would touch me so gently.
You would whisper promises
of always and forever in my ear,
but it was her name that lingered on your lips.
Maybe loving you was accepting
my participation ribbon while she held first prize.
But that was okay. I wasn't used to winning anyway.

THE LOST GIRLS

The greatest love story ever told
was never going to be us,
we were a pair of lines,
meeting at a single point
– clashing spectacularly
only to drift apart.
We went our separate ways
and yet I still find myself
thinking about you.
How we were once so close,
nothing hurts more than our almost.

LYRA WREN

Aphrodite came to me in my sleep
scented like salt water and desolation.
She watched me with saddened eyes
while tears slipped down my cheeks.

"Is love meant to be a painful thing?" I asked.

The goddess shrugged because she knew but
instead of speaking she only patted my head gently.

"How many more times will they break my heart?"
How much longer must I endure this pain?

It depends, she said quietly.
How much longer will you love them?

And all I could do was weep.

THE LOST GIRLS

Maybe in another world
we would have worked out
but we were just too different,
you and I. You were sun-kissed and
I was moon-blessed.
Both dappled in opposites.
I always cherished those moments
at dusk and dawn when we could both
burn brightly in the same sky.
In our next life, I hope we come back
as the stars we once wished on.

LYRA WREN

Tonight I am breathless and drunk
on what ifs as I often am when it comes to you.
What if I hadn't laughed at your joke that day?
It wasn't funny at all but the way you smiled
gave me butterflies and I was hooked on you.
What if we hadn't fallen in love?
Would I still feel tortured by this heartbreak?
And the worst *what if* of all:
What if we had gotten married?
Maybe on another night I'll be stone cold sober
and your name won't cross my mind.
But tonight I am tipsy on lost possibilities.

THE LOST GIRLS

Your ghost lingers in my mind.
It's been years since you left my bed
but your imprint still haunts the sheets.
Warm nights curled together whispering
visions of our future have grown sleepless.
I find myself swiping ceaselessly through
every other fish in the sea,
but you are there in every face.
And I wonder if you still think of me
when your arms are wrapped around her.
The cold echo of your hands was numbing
– a stark contrast to her warmth.
But in my dreams your phantom touch burned.
And I wished you'd haunt me forever.

LYRA WREN

The intimacy of dancing with strangers;
becoming faceless in a crowded place
with friends you will never meet again.
For moments you are a mystery
even to yourself. Given the gift
of anonymity for the night.
They may not know your favorite color
but you exchange dark secrets
that become buried in the shadows of the crowd.
And you seek solace in knowing
that your secrets will die with them,
as is the intimacy of strangers.

THE LOST GIRLS

Men claim women are frigid
when their cat calls disguised as
compliments go unanswered
but if women choose to sleep
with them, they are sluts.
We are not to be believed when
we make claims of abuse because
it could ruin *their* lives so we are
damned to be silent while we
swallow their sins against us.
Girls cannot win in a society
run by men which views females
as a fantasy made only for them.

LYRA WREN

Girls are meant to be mothers, they say,
handing us baby dolls instead of briefcases.
People insist on *some days* as though
motherhood is an inevitability but
we are more than our wombs
and having children should
always be our choice.

THE LOST GIRLS

Grief is many things but for me
it was so quiet that one could hear
the echoes of laughter left behind.
An unbearable absence lingered heavy
in my chest that no feeling could fill.
I didn't really know how to exist in a
world without you in it but somehow
each day I was growing around my anguish
until the emptiness didn't feel quite so heavy.
Some days I can barely breathe but more often
there are times that I can smile and laugh.
I don't think this hurt will ever go away
but I take comfort in knowing I must
have loved you a lot to feel this raw.

LYRA WREN

Hatred for my father lies
in my mother's eyes.
And in the right light
with my chin tilted
to the side, I look a little
like him and I wonder if
she hates that half of me.

THE LOST GIRLS

Birthdays are terribly heavy despite
the party balloons and pastel cake.
As a kid, you crave the attention and
the sugar rush that comes along with it.
Time is slow and full of sweet nostalgia
so you gather the years like peel-away stickers,
always speeding to collect the next one.
But then, you grow up and birthdays come
with frosted smiles and a melancholic gaze.
The clock chimes twelve times at midnight and
without knowing why, you begin to cry.
Nothing has really changed and you are still
the same person but it feels like a goodbye.

I'm caught in a battlefield
surrounded by corpses of who
I could have been and I wonder
how I was the one who crawled out
from that grave while parts of me
were buried deep within the dirt.
I am built from the girl who saw
a star in every firefly but I am also
built from the woman who saw
pieces of her dreams die.

THE LOST GIRLS

Second place. Second rate.
That's what she'd always been.
She never had the best grades
or the clearest skin.
And while she felt pretty
she'd never known beauty
in the eyes of those around her.
Yet there were moments where
she loved her life so deeply
she felt nothing less
than extraordinary.

The Mending

The girl laid on the beach
surrounded by the rocky seas
around her shore. As the salt water
stung her cheeks she could almost imagine
Aphrodite rising from the seafoam.
She wondered if those age old eyes
would hold pity for her. A lost girl
whose heart was filled with loneliness.
Though the love goddess emerged
from frozen waters, her hand was warm
when she gently touched the girl's chest
and whispered, *your greatest gift*
is finding peace within yourself.

THE LOST GIRLS

Do not praise her decay
for she is wasting away
trying to keep herself warm
with a can of empty calories.
She tries to make herself smaller
so she can fit in the frame of what
society says is pretty but in truth
she seeks to burrow in the space
between her ribs because it
falsely feels like control.
Do not tell your children that beauty
is buried in rock bottom. Do not hand
them a shovel because they will dig
their own grave. Tell them that you
love them and everything they are.
Tell them there is beauty in recovery.

I used to wish I could melt
right beneath the floorboards
if it meant people weren't looking
at me as if I was an object. A thing.
The first time a man looked down
my shirt, I was thirteen. Instead of
telling the man off, my dad told me
to cover up. I became acutely aware
of the shame I should feel in my
adolescent body. I am in my twenties now
and that shame is still reflected in some
people's eyes. But I stand steady on these
crooked boards even when my feet bleed.

THE LOST GIRLS

My therapist told me today
that my father swallows his pain.
That the bitterness sits heavy in
his stomach and festers like poison.

I don't tell her I think I must be rotten too.
Like dad. Like daughter. Everytime I look
at my father, there is only anger and pain
and I don't know if that will ever change.

But unlike my father, I will gut the venom
from my voice. I am doing the work and
making my choice. My future daughter
won't decay and his trauma ends with me.

Forgiving a father is quiet whispers
descending into rage wrapped neatly
in barbed wire. Our independence cannot
stand being in the same room but still
we work through rough conversations
with our voices drenched in tears.
And though some days I'm so angry
my hands tremble, we are slowly healing
and I am hopeful.

THE LOST GIRLS

Some days I am aware of my
womanhood in all the wrong ways.
I crumble beneath the pressure of
the male gaze while quietly insisting
that I am not a two-dimensional object.
I am a woman. I always have to explain that
they are *not* the same thing and deep down
I know that I am not a fantasy so I will carve
this message into the minds of men who view
women as a madonna created solely for them.

Deflower is such a cruel term
because she will continue to bloom
long after you are gone.
Her petals will not wilt if they
are plucked away by greedy hands.
Her body is not yours to triumph
and you will never take away her ability
to build stronger roots and blossom
far brighter than before.

THE LOST GIRLS

I often think of a younger me and the empathy
she deserved but never really received. I long
to tell her how intelligent she is and how brave
she has been. I want her to know that beauty
isn't just blonde hair and blue eyes and that the
boldness radiating from her makes her a visionary.
I often think of a younger me but never do I listen
to the echoes of the woman in years to come.
We are so hard on ourselves in the moment but
if I listen closely I can almost hear her whispers of
you deserve love too.

I hope someday I will believe her.

I stopped pouring my energy into people
and turned it towards me instead.
When I wake up each morning
I brew my coffee and make my bed,
taking the time to savor each task.
I've found magic in the mundane things
and apologies do not spill from my lips
as easily as they used to because
I'm no longer sorry that
I'm falling in love with myself again.

THE LOST GIRLS

I've always known that love is shown
at the kitchen table. Each meal cooked
becoming a deliberate act of care.
I'll peel apart mandarin oranges to share
amongst my siblings because we all love
the taste of citrus at sunrise. Each Christmas
we pull down the mixing bowls and bake
hundreds of cookies, filling the air with
adoration and something slightly sweet.
Food loses its luster when you move away
and all dining hall food begins to taste the same.
When all that surrounds me is homesickness
and heartbreak, my mom will fill the Tupperware
with my favorite food. Love can be felt but it can also
be tasted, and a piece of home will always belong at
my childhood kitchen table.

A mother's love is unconditional.
Since the beginning you've found
your home in her. When you cry,
she cradles you close and says
she loves you most. She always
laughs at your jokes even when
they really aren't that funny.
You find that you want to tell her
everything even if it's just what you
had for breakfast this morning.
Because no matter what you say,
she will listen. A mother's devotion
is limitless but your love for her
outnumbers the stars in the sky.

THE LOST GIRLS

To my inner child,

Each time I look in the mirror,
I do not recognize the pieces of you
in this fully grown body.
The world has told you to
pick your poison as if accepting
misery is inevitable in adulthood.
But each time I rediscover
my love for your favorite things
I can tell you are smiling
and I feel a little closer to you.

LYRA WREN

It was obvious the dove
was not meant for this universe.
Stars glittered in her eyes and
she held a tender gaze for the
world around her. As such, even
when she cried dewdrops slid down
her cheeks, as if the very earth wept with her.
She was who the great masters painted,
though not even the gods could capture her visage.
Each night, she dozed beneath her window,
drenched in moonlight, and she dreamt
of flying with feathers fading at her fingertips.

THE LOST GIRLS

When I was little I wore
a pink peacoat. Boys called it girly,
hurling the word like an insult
from their sharpened tongues.
And so I tucked the little pink coat
in the back of my closet,
wondering when my femininity
became a crime. Instead I turned to red,
a vibrant, confident color.
I became fiery and rejected its paler counterpart.
Many years later, I tuck my chin into my red scarf
and spot pink nail polish on the grocery store shelf.
Without thinking much about it,
I toss it into my basket with a smile,
remembering my favorite pink coat.
Who said I couldn't have both?

LYRA WREN

To my platonic soulmate,

Some people believe soulmates don't exist
but I know that's not true.
We were not meant to be lovers
but in all the friends I've had,
nobody fits me quite as well as you.
There were no tugs of our heartstrings,
or sparks in our chests,
but instead this feeling like I knew
who you were and what we were
even though we had never met.
The universe knew what to do,
when they placed you in my life.
because we weren't meant to be lovers,
we were just meant to be.

THE LOST GIRLS

A girl in the bar bathroom
applies glitter to my eyes.
I only met her a moment ago,
but she shares her stars
with the women around her
until we all gleam. She says
we are beautiful until we bleed
confidence and that
is the universal language of women.

LYRA WREN

Adulthood looks a bit like
listening to music in the grocery store
while checking which almond milk is on sale.
It's cooking brownies at 3 a.m because you can
but then missing your 8 a.m because you did.
You have your own apartment with your
baby blanket folded at the end of the bed
but before all of that, you were seventeen.
Learning lessons alongside familiar faces.
People say your adventures begin when
you've been gifted with your cap and gown.
But they must not know of the nights spent
driving around with your best friends.
The feeling of freedom when your windows
are rolled down and nobody can hear
the secrets you whisper to the wind.
Some days you'll think of lunch periods and labs.
You'll miss each snow day and delay. Or touch
the fabric of your prom dress, wincing when you think
of how your feet ached at the end of the night.
You'll remember this adventure and its ending
and be filled with the fumes of nostalgia.

THE LOST GIRLS

Happy birthday little girl
but why do you cry?
Tears spilling like diamonds
from your age worn eyes.

"It's not because I am sad,"
I softly insist, voice watery
but thick with wonder.

Then why? Why do you weep?

"Because I made it." I do not say that
somedays I did not think I would
but somehow I think they knew.

To my best friends,

No red ribbon of fate ties us together
but one day we linked our pinkies and
made our own eternal promise because
fate does not define our friendship.
I chose you with intention as much as
you chose me and that vow will not change
no matter the distance between us.
You've proved that home can be a person.
You've shown I have a home in many places.

THE LOST GIRLS

The first time you caught my eye
it was not love at first sight.
Instead a quiet curiosity was
planted in my chest and I knew
it was only a matter of time before
you sunk beneath my bones and
nurtured this deep seated familiarity
into a love so fierce that I would question
if I had ever been in love before.

I've been a romantic ever since
I was a little girl. Flipping through fairy tales
and trying to imagine that I was her.
The heroine with bright blue eyes
and a mischievous smile.
The one who drew people to her
without even trying. But in the end
fairy tales are fantasy, or that's what I believed
because then one day, you came to me.
It isn't always easy because sometimes
we fight and we've gone through hard times
but for the first time in forever
I can picture a happily ever after.

THE LOST GIRLS

In the apartment complex down the street
two strangers dance, hand in hand beneath
the citrine kitchen light. It's 2 a.m. and quiet
has settled over the city but for hours
they have gazed at each other over the rims
of their wine glasses. They have smiled over
silly aprons and misread recipes. And now,
they sway to the hum of jazz on their old stereo.
And I can picture us so perfectly in their place.
Years from now, I hope you hold me that gently
while the rest of the world sleeps around us.

LYRA WREN

Love was a materialistic being.
It never said I'm sorry or kissed my bruises.
But love bought me a new bike
and took me on a trip.
Love couldn't come see me for my birthday.
But love gave me a card filled with cash.

So maybe you can understand that,
when you spent hours making me a playlist
and read my favorite book,
when you held me under the stars
and told me it was okay to cry,
I didn't know love could be that too.

THE LOST GIRLS

"Does forever exist?" I asked you one night,
curled beneath the heavy weight of your arm.
Rain pattered on the rooftop,
permeating the air with its rich scent.

You hummed thoughtfully,
accompanied by the whir of the fan
working to gently blow the humidity from our skin.
"I hope so," you mused, hand outstretched
toward the open window.

"Why?" I wondered drowsily.
Moonlight gleamed through the rain,
fashioning stars beneath the clouds.

"Because," you whispered, "I don't think this life
would be enough time for me to love you."
We nestled closely into the sheets
and the rain continued to fall.

The day I knew I loved you
we were sleep drunk and
slumped together by the kitchen window,
watching the morning sun
crawl over the horizon line.
But even as the sunrise
stained the trees pink,
I couldn't help but notice the way
dawn's light kissed your skin,
casting a golden halo
through your tousled hair.
And that's when I knew
that no sunrise could ever
beat the sight of you.

THE LOST GIRLS

I still wish on birthday candles
and shooting stars. I drop pennies
in wishing wells and search the fields
for four leaf clovers because people
can think it's silly and dumb
but is it so bad to want prosperity
in a world with so much pain.

One day I won't wake
in my mother's house
on the holidays and
the smell of her baking
won't lure me from
my childhood bedroom.
I will ache at the realization
that no sisters are waiting
for me at the kitchen table.
But today, as a reminder
I will hold them a little tighter.

THE LOST GIRLS

I sculpted myself out of clay today.
Ran my thumbs over the ridges of my
brow and beneath my smiling mouth.
Spent hours carving the curve of my
nose just right. And though I saw my
mother in my eyes and my father in
my jawline, it all came together to be me.
And for a moment, I held my face in my
hands and caressed my cheeks and it was
undeniably art but it felt a little more like love.

LYRA WREN

In my dreams I am young again,
releasing fireflies from the palm
of my hands. I wished on them
as if they were stars and watched
as they joined the cosmos once more.

I woke with a soft smile and tears
on my cheeks then watched the
night sky from my bedroom window
wrapped in a warm blanket of nostalgia.

Adulthood is hard. It threatens to drain you
but I've found it's about rediscovery too.
It is finding out fireflies are not stars
but daring to dream on them anyway.

THE LOST GIRLS

I don't need a compass or map
to tell me the right way because
in life, there is no such thing.
We make up the journey as we go
and maybe it's better not to know.

They will tell lost girls to find
their own way but they will still
try to tell you the correct path to take.
I used to be so afraid of making mistakes
that I followed their directions to be safe.

But I am older now and a bit wiser.
And I'm learning how to reignite my fire.
I will burn their atlas away because
I'll always be a little lost and that's okay.

There once was a weaver
who wove pages of poetry.
With ink-stained fingers,
she spun her syllables
and stitched them together
until the words formed prose
that even Apollo would envy.

Special Acknowledgments

I. *To my sisters,*
whom I will always share my oranges with

II. *To my mom,*
who loved me, supported me and saved me

III. *To my dad,*
who gave me life lessons in forgiveness

IV. *To my best friends,*
who believed in me and this book

V. *To my readers,*
who put the pen in my hand again

About The Author

Lyra Wren is a poet and storyteller born and raised in Indiana. She's been a creative ever since she was a little girl whether that was doodling in the empty spaces of her homework or writing countless stories for her family to read. She has a bachelor's in studio art at Indiana University. When she isn't writing in the cafe of her local bookstore, Lyra spends much of her time painting, reading, enjoying the outdoors, curating Spotify playlists and perusing astrological charts.

In 2021, Lyra began posting her poetry to TikTok and she has since grown her online following into a large, supportive community. She strives to bring comfort, hope and understanding to her audience and make the world a place where people feel a bit less alone.

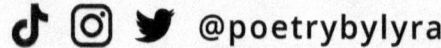 @poetrybylyra

@canned.spaghettio

About The Book

The Lost Girls is a collection of poetry dealing
with themes of girlhood and growing up.
But more than that, it is a lens into my life.
It is split into four sections:
The Beginning, The Becoming,
The Breaking and The Mending.
Each chapter deals with a different period
of my life from childhood to adulthood.

For years I've wanted to tell my story,
not because it is unique but because it isn't.
We are all stumbling our way through life,
dealing with heartbreak, love, grief, family,
mental health, loneliness and feeling lost.
Nobody has all of the answers and that's okay.

The Lost Girls takes readers through the ups
and downs of life. It reminds us to find
joy in the journey and the little things.
It reminds us to engage with our emotions
– even when it hurts. It reminds us that
life is about discovery and rediscovery.
It reminds us that it's normal to feel lost.
It reminds us that fireflies are not stars,
but that it is okay to dream on them anyway.